The Greeks

Text by
Victor Duruy
Translated by John Christmas

Crescent Books
New York

First English edition published by Editions Minerva S.A., Genève
Copyright © MCMLXXX by Editions Minerva S.A., Genève All rights rese
ISBN : 0-517-323427
This edition is published by Crescent Books, a division of Crown Publishers
a b c d e f g h   Printed in

Above, the islands which can be seen from Cape Sounion, not far from Athens. Left, one of the monuments of the Palace of Cnossos — the symbol of the ancient Cretan civilization. Below, figures from the archaic period.

"What do you mean by Greece?" Philip of Macedonia ironically asked the Aetolians when they reproached him for being a barbarian king. "Where are its boundaries? And are most of you Greek?"

This name had the same sort of history as that of Italy: both traveled from one end to the other of a peninsula which later took the name to designate its entirety. Dodona, a small canton of Epirus, first used the name; but gradually it spread as far as Thessaly, the region south of Thermopylae, and the Peloponnesus. Still later, it included Epirus, Illyria as far as Epidamnus, and finally Macedonia. Another curious point is that the name *Greece* was unknown in Greece: it was called *Hellas,* the land of the Hellenes, and we do not know what reasoning was behind the choice of the world *Graecia* in the Roman language.

Taken on the whole, Greece was not fertile enough to nourish an idle population, nor was it so poor that its inhabitants had to spend all their energy searching for their means of subsistence. The diversity of its landscape of plains and mountains, and of its climate, varying from the snows of the Pindus to the almost Asiatic croplands of the Peloponnesus presented the Greeks with precisely the variety of challenges which develops the faculties and creates a wealth of ideas from an abundance of knowledge—in other words, a civilization. More than any other people, the Greeks were required by the nature of their land to be shepherds, farmers and also merchants.

And like their land they had a severe nature, making them active and muscular. Their broad chests were those of the deep-breathing men of the mountains; although they were not especially tall, they were powerful in physical combat, resistant to fatigue, and fast on their legs; after assuring their own independence, these military qualities made them rulers of Asia. Nature had graced them with beautiful faces; life in the open air and continual exercise developed the elegant proportions of their bodies, and artists had only to look around them for models.

And that was not all: in this variegated land, where no two valleys are

Below, the famous Lion Gate at Mycenae. This page, the head of an idol (marble, Cycladic art). Bottom, sculpture of the same period. Right, female figure (Cycladic art, 3rd millenium BC). Following pages: panoramic view of Mycenae.

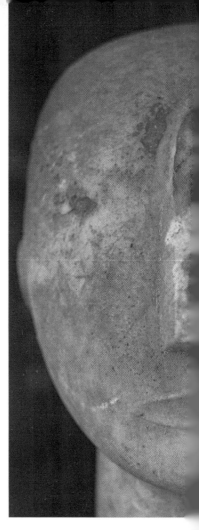

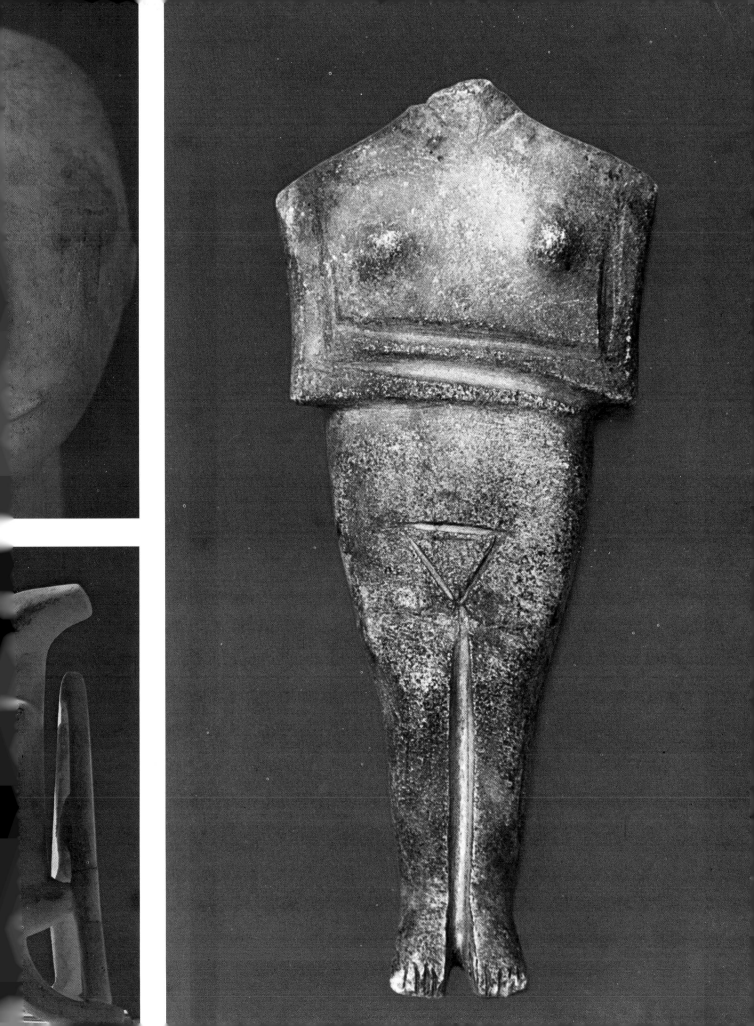

Left, overall view of the Palace of Minos at Cnossos. Bottom, the throne-room in the palace. This page, the face of Apollo (archaic statuette). Below, the partly renovated façade of the Palace of Cnossos.

alike, there was an equal variety of customs and institutions, producing a universal restlessness, in market places as in minds, and everywhere a sense of effort and striving. No other people has lived quite as fully as the Greeks.

The faults and advantages of the land, plus its coastline, where earth and sea meet harmoniously, are perfectly summarized in one of Greece's regions: this is Attica, with the fertile soil of Marathon and Eleusis producing a ratio of sixty to one, with its olive trees and perfumed honey of Hymettus, its Pentelic marble and Mount Laurium mines, its air so clear that one could supposedly see Mineva's aigrette and spear on the Acropolis all the way from Cape Sounion; and in addition to this, there is the sea bounding the region on three sides. When the Athenians climbed to the top of the Parthenon, they could see these numerous islands scattered around them among the sea's waves, a naturally inviting domain, pointing the way to the shores of Thrace, Asia and Egypt. Each morning the north wind rose to carry their ships gently to the Cyclades; each night the opposing wind brought them back to port under a starlit sky. "Sweet and soft is our air." said an Athenian poet, "winter is without harshness for us, and never are we harmed by the rays of Phœbus."

During the heroic age of Greece, customs were simple because people were not rich; yet they enjoyed a freedom which was quite unknown in the Orient. At this time there was virtually no servile class: those who had been taken prisoner in war or purchased were less slaves than servants. The dying Alcestis held out his hand to his slaves for the last farewell. Emmaeus hoped that Ulysses, coming back to Ithaca, would grant him a house, a piece of land and a wife, and, upon meeting his master's son, would kiss his forehead and eyes; but, even then, the old shepherd said what all Greece, even its philosophers, was to say later: "The gods take away half of a man's qualities the day they make him a slave".

The slave's position was an easy one, and that of women was honored. Here domestic society, the family, was better established than among the oriental peoples, excepting the Jews; this in turn provided a guarantee that political society would also be more soundly constituted, with greater freedom and justice. Polygamy was forbidden, but not concubinage. While the Greek woman was still purchased, she was nevertheless no longer condemned to the obscurity and solitude of the harem; she lived openly, at least in earlier times; later her existence would seem more harsh: in Athens she would be locked in the gynaeceum or women's quarters, and would remain in an inferior legal position to her husband. Being excluded from her husband's inheritance, and legally the ward of her sons, she was permanently a minor. The links of the chain that formerly bound her in servitude were not all broken. And yet her lot was to improve since the dowry which would become her property would assure her future. Laërtes bought Eurycleia, "but," says Homer, "though she was very young, he did not make her his companion, fearing his wife." Since the hero did not disdain manual labor, the woman was thus left with the domestic chores. Even the king's daughters drew water from the fountains, as did the beautiful

A detail of the Parthenon.

On these two pages, specimens of the three great orders of Greek architecture: Doric (above), Ionic (below) and Corinthian (right).

Nausicaa, and Polyxena, Priam's daughter. Andromache fed Hector's horses; Helen worked at marvelous embroideries; and Penelope could calm the suitors' patience only by showing them the last garment she was preparing for the old Laërtes, this fabric which she wove during the day and undid at night: "What would the women of Greece say if I left this hero without a shroud when the Fates carry him to his death?"

However, in this age when strength and daring were honored, infidelity was not an unpardonable crime. The adulterer was never very severely punished. The guilty wife was merely disgraced: she could no longer wear certain ornaments nor attend public sacrifices. If she did not obey these rules, she was liable to have her other ornaments and clothing torn from her, and could be struck but not injured.

The notion of moral law is not to be found in Homer — but neither is that of eroticism. At least the poet's contemporaries did not know the depraved activities later to be introduced by Asia and the gymnastic institutions. Woman was the single object of man's affections; but for her, love was restrained to the desires created in her by Aphrodite's girdle, "where we find all the charms and words that capture even the soul of the wise man." Violent passions aroused by love were of another age, and were to be sung by other poets.

From the great mass of Arcadia's mountains, the Taygetus and Parnon ranges break away and stretch to the south as far as Cape Teanarus and Cape Malea, which are often struck by storms. "When you go around Cape Malea," the sailors said, "forget everything you've left at home." Between these two

Below, the remains of a temple dedicated to Demeter. Right, the temple of Hera at Paestum.

Above, detail of the monument known as the Athenian Treasure, at Delphi. Right, the grandiose setting of Delphi.

mountain chains flows the Eurotas River, rushing below Sparta, where it meets a slightly inclined plain which slows down its course as it continues to the sea.

A valley, closed in by the wall-like slopes of the surrounding mountains, irregularly broken by numerous hills, and in summer burned by the almost tropical sun, unaffected by sea winds while above we can see the peaks of Taygetus, often covered with snow: this is the Lacedaemon Valley.

The character and climate of this region naturally produced energetic, hardy men; the land is not infertile, but it yields its fruits only in return for painful labors.

Lycurgus was Sparta's great man. Research and historical analysis have not been able to dispel the many uncertainties which revolve around him.

It is believed he was born in the 9th century B.C., the son of King Eunomos who was stabbed while trying to break up a fight and then died of his wounds. His older brother also met an untimely death, and Lycurgus was king until the pregnancy of the queen, his sister-in-law, was noticed; she offered to destroy the child if he would marry her. But Lycurgus outwitted her and saved his brother's son. The lords, irritated by his wise administration during Charilaos' childhood, forced him into exile. He traveled for a long time, studying with wise men and learning the habits of foreign countries. On Crete he was instructed in the laws of Minos by a poet who sung his verses accompanied by a lyre, later calling him to Sparta to help calm the spirits. From Asia Minor he took only the poetry of Homer, but Egyptian priests counted him among their disciples. Later Spartans said that he went as far as India to learn the ancient wisdom of the

16

Brahmins. These were long and difficult trips for the men of those times; in actual fact however, Lycurgus did not make them, and Indian priests taught him nothing.

Upon his return, after an absence which supposedly lasted eighteen years, Lycurgus found Sparta in great trouble; the people themselves felt a great need for reform. Thus the moment was favorable. In order to add the name of Delphic Apollo, the national god, to his own authority, he consulted the oracle on his projects. Pythia hailed him in the name of Jupiter. Strengthened by the god's support, whether earned or bought, Lycurgus began by interesting a numerous and powerful group in his plans.

The senate was composed of thirty members. It deliberated on proposals

Above, the sanctuary of Athena at Delphi, one of the most famous of all Greek temples.

Right, the sacred way at Delphi and the pediment of the temple of Hera at Paestum.

to present to the population and judged criminal cases. Its members were elected in a highly unusual way: the candidates filed past the people one by one, and each was received with greater or lesser cheers. Elders, shut in a neighboring chamber from which they could see nothing, noted those who were received with the greatest cheers, and these were then declared senators. Named for life, they were irremovable and accountable to no-one — a fact which contributed greatly to their aristocratic standing. The major concern of the legislators and politicians of antiquity was to keep the city within its framework, ensuring that it neither shrank nor expanded. But among a small warlike people, where each citizen was an active soldier, fighting could have the effect of limiting the size of

the population. Ways had to be found to prevent an undue decline in numbers: legislation was therefore enacted to penalize celibacy and to heap disgrace on those citizens who failed to produce offspring. For example, one day Dercyllidas, a distinguished general, went before an assembly; a young Lacedaemonian did not rise as he approached, though custom required that he should do so. The old warrior was astonished.

"You have no children," says the young man, "who can one day pay me the same honor." He was not considered guilty. Later on the government gave rewards to the citizens with the greatest number of children, and favored adoptions and marriages between wealthy heiresses and poor citizens. Kings who had to sanction all adoptions and arranged the marriages of orphans when the father had not made his own will known, could also, for a certain time, save a useful citizen from poverty and prevent an accumulation of wealth in the same hands.

Thus, each citizen owed the nation children. In the case of a sterile union, a wife could be loaned to fulfil one's obligation to give the state its future soldiers, a debt in which the children belonged more to the city than to the father. Leaving the mother's breast, the young Spartan fell into the hands of the state; the father had to bring him to the Leschia, the meeting place of the elders. Hopelessly he would try to save his son: if the elders found him weak or unfit, he was thrown from the top of Mount Taygetus, and the poor child was punished by death the first day of his life for not seeming likely to become a sturdy enough

Above, overall view of the Acropolis, from the side of the Propylaea. Right, another view of the Propylaea and one of the foundation walls of the Acropolis.

Following pages: a) aerial view of the temple of Concord at Agrigento; b) aerial view of the Greek monuments at Paestum, with, on the left, the temple of Neptune, and on the right the basilica.

warrior, — a cruel and monstrous custom accepted as a necessity by philosophers and politicians starting with Plato and Aristotle!

After this terrible inspection of those who were forced to be part of it, the state gave the child back to his mother and allowed him to remain with her until he was seven years old; at this age it then reclaimed him, never again to release him, and from this moment on, the child's life was a long trial of patience, sobriety and even suffering. He was immediately placed in a troop which teachers, chosen from among the best of the young men, directed under the surveillance of an officer called a *pedonome*. They were trained in the palaestra or gymnasium, in running and the use of weapons, anything that would increase the force and agility of their bodies; their minds were trained in courage and patience. "You will have great difficulty," said Xenophon, "in finding better formed men and more lissom bodies than the Spartans: they give equal care to the exercising of the neck, the hands and the legs. They wear no shoes, and the same garment is worn summer and winter; for a bed they use reeds they themselves cut in the Eurotas; they are given little nourishment in order to force them to pilfer by cunning and shrewdness what they must to satisfy their appetites." It is unusual to see theft taught in such a way; but because of the

Left, the ancient theater of Delos.
Bottom, view of the theater at Delphi.

society uniting the Spartans, it was not truly theft. Anyone who allowed himself to be caught was punished, not for committing a wrongful act, but for bungling it. When tracking the enemy in actual warfare as adults, they would thus remember the clever ploys which they had learned as children for finding food. In order that they would become able to withstand great suffering they were made to undergo some very severe ordeals; they were also beaten with rods at the altar of Diana, the one best enduring the pain being awarded the title of "victor of the altar".

The education of Lacedaemonian girls was only slightly less grueling. Instead of being condemned to a sedentary life in the gynaeceum, women slaves were made to spin wool and make clothes; young Spartan girls had to prepare themselves for the day when they would be required to give robust children to the nation. For young men and women alike there were exercises for the body, races and wrestling, to keep them healthy and strong. The Phenomerides engaged in these activities in public while nearly naked until they were twenty years old—the normal age for marriage. The Spartans were of necessity strong-willed and austere of habit. There was no luxury: this principle was maintained by the use of iron coins, valid only in the region, which were especially made so heavy that a chariot was needed to transport even a small amount.

Commerce, like the luxury which it led to, was shunned. Foreigners would have brought in new ideas: they were in fact forbidden to enter Sparta, except on certain days. Nor could a Spartan travel outside the region without official permission, and the death penalty was prescribed for those who tried to live in some other land: they were deserters.

The same principle was applied to the institution of common meals,

Top left, remains of the columns of the temple of Athena, at Priena. Above, one of the columns of the Parthenon. Facing, the remains of Olympia.

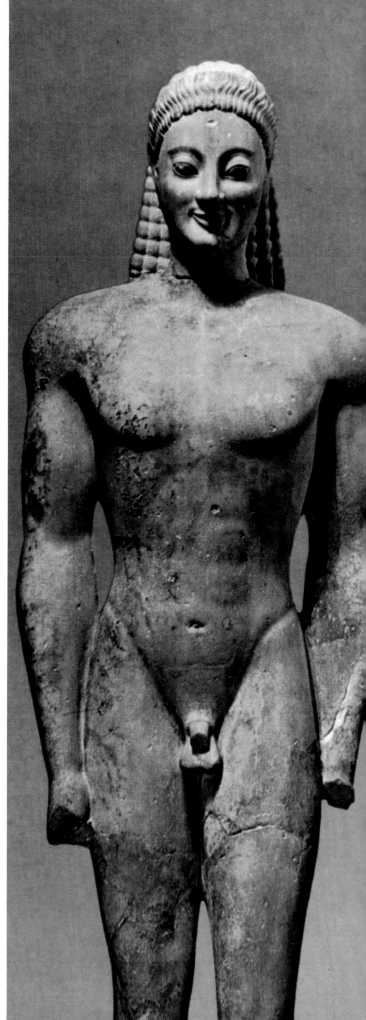

Above, a young Athenian performing gymnastic exercises. Below, typical hairdo (Curos of Milo).

which all Spartans, even kings, were obliged to attend, or risk losing their political rights; absences were, however, excused in the case of a sacrifice or a prolonged hunt, which promised the guests a present for the feast. These meals, called *phidities,* were strict; each man was provided with an equal amount of barley flour, wine, wheat, figs, and a small share of seasoning or meat. One could add to this only hunted game or a part of the sacrifices burned for the gods. Anyone who was so poor as to bring nothing was excluded from the tables and lost his rights as a citizen.

The dish which began the meal was the black broth which made Dionysius of Syracuse make a face. "Something is really missing in here," he said to the cook who had prepared it for him. "What then?" "Your having gone for a swim in the Eurotas." Old men as well as children attended these meals; heroic deeds were praised here, and shameful actions were scorned all, with sharp but friendly mockery.

In times of war, guests at the same table became soldiers in the same regiment, so that each man, fighting in sight of his friends, was encouraged and strengthened.

Each citizen could punish the children of another citizen. When necessary, one could borrow a neighbors' slaves, his hunting dogs, or his horses, on the condition that one returned everything to its place in the same state that one had found it in. The Spartans sometimes went so far in the sacrifice of personal property that they were greatly admired by Xenophon, and would have been especially repellent to us with our ideas on the sanctity of family ties.

The small region separated from central Greece by imposing mountains and which stretches out in a promontory into the Aegean Sea, bounded on the right by Euboea, on the left by the smaller islands of Salamis and Aegina, is Attica, the most justly celebrated place in the world in the history of the human mind. It is divided into three, semi-circular basins, the plains of Eleusis, Athens and Marathon. The genius of the inhabitants, shaped by the location of the area, historical circumstances and a climate of a sweet spring and a clement winter, differed profoundly from the Spartan character: open and vast like the limitless horizon seen from the Acropolis, drawing the eye far out into the Aegean; lively and sharp like the sea breeze which ruffles the purpled hills of Attica; inquisitive, bold and industrious, as is often true of people living in coastal regions, exposed to foreign contacts, or of those whose territory does not provide them with enough living space; and lastly, endlessly kept on guard by the multiplicity of impressions received through the pure and sonorous air during transparent nights, which are not the darkness of shadow, but rather the absence of daylight. The Athenians were well-balanced because of the very nature of their land, where nothing was to be found in abundance; but even more important was the fact that they had a well-balanced mind.

"Land with the long coastline"—this is the meaning of the name Attica, open to the sea on three sides, receiving from there and from the routes of the Boeotian mountains inhabitants of very different origins. Each group took up separate quarters and refused to have anything in common with the others.

Left, classical stele and archaic statuette: two typical specimens of Greek beauty as seen by the Greeks.

Much time and effort was needed to reduce these many states to twelve, to unite them through marriages, and to have them bring their disputes before a common tribunal. This first union was called in legend Cecrops; the second, in which twelve villages made up a single city and political unit after each civil unit, was called Theseus.

Later on in Athens there was to be found a man who lived without public honors amidst the crowd of fellow-citizens. In his youth he had devoted himself to trade to make up for the injustice of his inheritance as arranged by his father. He had traveled a great deal, hoping, at the same time to find, among the many peoples who passed before his eyes, his fortune through commerce and learning by the study of conduct and things. He had the reputation of a wise man, but a moderate wise man, who did not disdain the good things in life, good cheer and love, who even sang its pleasures in rather light verses, mixed, it is true, with good and profound maxims: his name was Solon.

Solon's genius was basically human, as was the Constitution he undertook to give to Athens.

There were three parties in the city: the men of the mountains, who wanted to change everything; the *paralians,* who wanted to change a few things; and the *pedians,* who did not want to change anything. Won over by Solon's moderation, they all agreed to put powers, responsibilities and revenues in his hands, in a word to give him dictatorship while he created the State (595). His

Above, figure from the classical period.
Left, head of the figure known as the Rampin Horseman (from the name of the first owner of the statue). Right, statuette of young girl.

friends urged him to maintain the dictatorship, and to make himself a tyrant rather than a law-maker; he responded with sharp comments and continued his work.

The Greek gods were forces of Nature or the manifestations of moral or physical activity; but they were also good or bad men, just as we are; and it is because they represent humanity that they lived so long a time.

Herodotus regarded the poems of Homer and Hesiod as the source of all religious beliefs in Greece. The amiable narrator tells us that he posed these impertinent questions to the priestesses of Dodona: "Where did each god come from? Did they all exist always? What shape do they take?" And he adds: "It is only recently that one has been able to answer these questions, perhaps because Homer and Hesiod are barely four hundred years older than me. And it is they who created the theogony of the Greeks, giving them their names, their honors and their forms."

Among the rites and legends of heroes and gods, we find the oldest worship of forests, the adoration of mountains, rocks, winds, and rivers. Agamemnon, in the Iliad, still invokes them like great divinities, and Achilles offers his fine head of hair to the Simois River. During the entire life of Hellenism, the oak was consecrated to Jupiter, the laurel to Apollo, the olive tree

Above, the famous low relief known as the Exaltation of the Flower. Right, in the Kerameikos of Athens: a funerary monument of the 4th century BC, in which the deceased, who was killed while fighting Corinth, is shown striking his enemy.

to Athena, the myrtle to Aphrodite, etc. Serpents, after having played a threatening role in earlier times, became the beneficent spirits at Delphi, Epidaurus and Athens. Lastly, certain rocks had divine images. Thus Herakles was represented at Hyettos in Boeotia by an uncut stone; Jupiter at Tegea by a triangular rock; and there were many others.

The beliefs of primitive times also involved the worship of fire: that which burned in the home, those of the gods' altars and the States, and that which sprang mysteriously from the depths of volcanic lands.

There are two kinds of religion: those revealed in a Holy Book, and those of Nature. Jews, Christians and Moslems have the former, while the Orient and Greece have the latter, delving into the heart of Nature, from which there flows the great current of universal life. In the great faiths which originated in the Sinai, Jerusalem and Mecca, religious development came from prophets, interpreting a sacred text; in Greece, the interpreters of revelation were poets.

The Phoenicians of Sidon spread the worship of their protective divinity, Astarte or Aphrodite; her image decorated the prows of their ships, to protect them from the waves, — a notion which the Greeks poetically expressed by saying that Aphrodite was born on the white foam of the briny deep. From

Below, the famous Venus of Milo, the glory of Greek statuary. Right, statue of a woman (5th century) and of a butcher. Following pages: detail of a frieze from the Parthenon.

Ascalon she passed to Cyprus, and from there to Cythera, "the empurpled island," where the Phoenicians built a temple to her. But her worship spread slowly: in the Homeric period it was still quite restricted. Later, the Syrian goddess, having become the goddess of love, was the most charming creation of the religious spirit of the Greeks; she had altars everywhere, images embodying the perfect feminine beauty, and too many worshippers.

Poseidon or Neptune, the god of the sea, who demanded human sacrifices and the burning of horses, must be one of the country's oldest divinities, undoubtedly brought by the Greeks from Asia and the islands along with Rhea, the Phrygian Cybele, and Minerva (Athena). The former never played anything but a minor role in Greece, while the latter had as her symbol the olive tree, native to the Asian coasts. Olympia and Athena seem to have worshipped Poseidon earlier in a particular religion, and the Ionians considered him their national god; in Asia, general assemblies were held in his temple. On the other hand, he was not held in great honor by the Dorians, except at Corinth. Earlier legends naturally made Poseidon the husband of Demeter: the humid element fertilizing the land. At first Athena was not the symbol of the moral qualities later represented by Minerva, but a personification of the waters; this naturally connected her with Poseidon, not however by marriage, since being sterile as the briny deep she remained a barren virgin. Later she was the divinity of war whom Homer shows us covering heroes with her shield on the battlefield. But it was

Below, at Olympia, the entrance to the studio of the great sculptor Phidias. Right, low relief showing a scene from domestic life.

inevitable that the goddess of the incorruptible waters and the impalpable air should become also that of chastity and moral purity, when Greek polytheism, escaping from naturalism by the progress of ideas, became more spiritual by substituting for the personification of the deadly forces of matter the moral qualities vested in the gods as they were gradually discovered in man himself. Thus Pallas-Athena, having sprung from Jupiter's brain, like his divine thought, became the industrious goddess and the intelligent force which nothing could resist.

Dionysus (Bacchus), the god of the vine, had first appeared on the island of Naxos, and was forever worshipped by the Thracians; Artemis (Diana), with her homicidal cult and Amazon-like savagery, who had a famous sanctuary at Ephesus, and much-dreaded altars at Tauris; lastly Ares (Mars), the god of carnage and perhaps Thrace's principal divinity: all these were evidently of foreign origin.

But the most important of these religious novelties was the late introduction into Greece of the worship of Apollo, the eternally young and beautiful god, personification of the radiant light he created.

The first altars to Apollo in Hellas were built on Olympus and the rock of Delos. A third, which became far more famous than the other two, was the one which the Cretans were thought to have built in his honor at Cryssa, on the Gulf of Corinth, later transported to the cliffs of Parnassus, a majestic site, more conducive to the safety of the priests and the faith of the pilgrims. When the Olympic Dorians established themselves near Phocis, they confusedly gave the same veneration to the sanctuaries of Delphi and Tempe, and each year a religious procession went from one to the other.

Thus Apollo became the great divinity of both parts of the Hellenic world, from the Ionians of Delos to the Dorians at Delphi, and pre-eminently the civilizing god of Greece, the destroyer of monsters (Python), the one who, more than any other, demanded physical and moral purity; who, surrounded by the chorus of the Muses and the Graces, charmed the immortals by his songs and the sounds of his lyre, revealed future things to man, and struck the wicked with his golden arrow. "I will love," cries the son of the beautiful Latona, "I will love the pleasing zither and the bent bow, and I will announce Zeus' plans to the mortals."

Under the influence of ideas connected with the worship of Apollo, a greater civilization was born and a new age of Greek life began. Society was better organized; urban life expanded and temples were raised to the gods. Songs and music replaced savage cries. The gods drew nearer to man and revealed their plans in the oracles, since Zeus had given Apollo divine inspiration and seated him on the prophetic throne. The guilty were no longer condemned to a sure death, and crime was no longer a hereditary stigma necessitating the punishment of future generations. Atonement wiped out sin. This was a world of harmony, light, intelligence and grace, replacing that of chaos, shadows, power and terror. Delphi was its center, as it was the center of the universe, and from there the gods spread over the Hellenic people the inspiration for verse, music and the arts, as well as the never-ending revelation of divine thought.

The Gorgon's head (ruins of Didimae).

All the Hellenic tribes adopted the cult of Apollo; and at the foot of his altars, in common prayer and faith, men of Dorian stock and Ionian Greeks met. Sparta did nothing without consulting his oracle at Delphi, and Athens, along with all of Ionia, honored him at Delos by solemn festivities.

Even greater honors awaited the god of Delphi in the last days of paganism, when the emperor Aurelian called him the *Deus certus,* and Julian made him the king of the sky and the world. But even before them, Pindar had already given him some of the characteristics of a Mosaic Jehovah: "God almighty," he said, "you know the end of all and the ways of all things; you know the number of the leaves which blossom in the springtime, and of the grains of sand that the waves and impetuous winds roll about in the sea; you see what must be and what will be its cause." The idea of monotheism floated vaguely in the midst of polytheistic clouds.

The divinities with the greatest number of worshippers were the twelve gods of Olympus, whose control was restricted and whose functions were defined by the later theogony: Zeus, the supreme god, obeyed by all the others, the protector of the entire Hellenic race, who, like the Mosaic Jehovah, was also called the Most High;

Juno or Hera, the queen of the sky, whose symbol was the peacock, because its brilliant eyes and spread plumage was a reminder of the stellar firmament;

Poseidon, the god of the waters; Apollo, the sun which lights and the intelligence which inspires; Athena, wisdom and science, who gives men prudent thoughts, and teaches women beautiful works and wise resolutions; Aphrodite, beauty, Ares, war; Hephaestus, the useful arts; the chaste Hestia, who presided over the domestic virtues; Demeter, who ripened the harvests; Artemis, "the divine sister of Phoebus," like him, both unmarried and the "friend of rapid arrows." Hermes, whose original nature is unclear, but who early on must have given men contrived eloquence and a capacity for guile, lying and daring acts of

Top left, a frieze from the Parthenon. Bottom, low relief showing domestic life and characteristic detail of a human body, on another low relief. Above, wrestling scene.

45

larceny— valuable qualities in barbaric times. Homer had already made him the messenger of the gods; he also led the dead, and perhaps in this double duty, was the personification of the wind which brought the divine words from far away, and carried the poor dried leaves of souls to the subterranean abyss. But why and how did he later become the ithyphallic Hermes, and later divine Reason, the Logos sent to earth by the gods? Different times give the same name to very different things, and the history of religion is full of such transformations which are one of the conditons of their vitality.

Above all the gods of Hellenic Olympus reigned Destiny, a god without life, without legend, even without form, who on earth had no altar and who, from the depths of the Empyrean where he was inaccessible by prayer, maintained the world's moral equilibrium and kept it safe from the caprices of the other deities. This god who distributed to each person his lot of good and evil had been created, or rather was born from man's troubled conscience, to explain the inexplicable and to make understood the incomprehensible, that is, the distant and hidden causes of events and the superior motives which carried them out. When describing some iniquity he did not understand, Herodotus would see in it a divine act and simply bow to it.

All the divinities, including Zeus himself, were subject to the law of Destiny.

In ancient times, when natural phenomena sharply struck men's imaginations, the art of reading the entrails of victims and of interpreting dreams, the flight of birds and flashes of lightning, were all part of religion and politics: thus Tiresias and Calchas were in good standing with the kings. Then with the progress of secular wisdom, more attention was given to the affairs of the earth than the sky.

Plato said, "God gave man divination to make up for his lack of intelligence." So it was not the most cultivated mind which received the privilege of lifting the veil from the future. The blind man and the madman became infallible prophets for the mob. Fountains whose waters disturbed the harmony of the human body or the spirit, and grottoes from which gas escaped, producing delirium and hallucinations, were considered places where the divinity was constantly present.

The fountain of Castalia, falling limpid and pure from the Phaedrial rocks, was holy water in which all who came to consult the oracle were purified.

If we exclude the prophetic oaks of Dodona in Epirus, whose priestesses read the noises in the winds of storms, there were no oracles in Greece more famous than the cave of Trophonios in Boeotia, and the Delphic temple in Phocis; both were created from a similar source, gaseous fumes read by a priestess or consultant. Plutarch and above all Pausanias have passed on to us the reports of strange scenes whose theatre was the sanctuary of Trophonios.

The mouth of the abyss, reminiscent of the one where Apollo killed the Python, was situated in a grotto which was less than three yards high and two yards wide. After long preparations and a rigorous examination, one descended into the grotto at night, with the aid of a ladder. At a certain depth, there was only an extremely narrow opening into which one slipped one's feet; one was then rushed with extreme speed to the bottom of the pit, bordering on a great abyss. Overcome by dizziness from the rapid movement, fear and the effect of the gas, one heard terrifying sounds, confused moans and voices which, in the

Above, the famous victory of Samothrace and, facing, a statue of Pythagoras.

Right, the famous Aphrodite of Cnide.

46

midst of the noises answered questions; or one saw strange apparitions, gleams of light among the shadows, and images which were also regarded as answers. With one's imagination overcome by these illusions one was dragged up, feet first, with the same force and speed as in the descent.

Apollo was less dreadful. For this god of light, interpreter of the will of Zeus, master of men and immortals, everything happened during the day. The authority of his oracles spread beyond the boundaries of the Hellenic world, as far as Lydia, and among the Etruscans, and to Rome, where the books of the Apollonian Cumaean Sibyl were so highly regarded. Cicero called it the earth's oracle, and Delphi was really the center of Hellenic religion, by virtue of the large number of pilgrims and the importance of the oracular consultations requested of the god who seemed to be present at this spot more than at any other sanctuary.

In order that the divine deed should seem more evident, Apollo's answers were originally repeated by a simple and unlearned young girl, almost always troubled by one of the nervous disorders which seem common in certain parts of Greece, and later on by a woman at least fifty years old; finally, a single Pythia was not sufficient to pronounce to the great number of pilgrims, and three of them were established. These unfortunate women were dragged, drooping and bewildered, to an opening in the earth from which certain vapors escaped. There, seated on a tripod, forcefully held there by priests, they received the prophetic exhalations. Their faces paled, their limbs shook with convulsive movements. At first they uttered only whimpering complaints and groans; soon, with gleaming eyes and foaming mouth, their hair on end with fright, they were heard to speak, amidst cries of pain, broken incoherent words, recorded with care and painstakingly put into verse by a priest, himself taken in by his faith in the oracle, who had to discover the revelation of the future as hidden in these words by the god. Thanks to the great number of pilgrims, the priests could keep themselves up to date on all that was happening in the States, and among individuals. What they learned in this way enabled them to give these inarticulate sounds a meaning which fear or hope made acceptable, and which was often made to come true by the sheer power of faith.

The Greeks loved oracles. A curious and impatient people, they wanted to know everything, even the future. Enigma pleased them, and called their subtle minds into play; but they also loved the pomp and magnificence of festivals, so brilliant under their beautiful sky, and they marked with religious solemnities the great stages of their national existence, as they did the natural and moral phenomena which appeared to them as a favor, counsel or threat from the gods.

In addition to the religious reason, Plato found a special motive for these solemnities: "The gods", he said, "being touched with compassion for men, condemned by nature to work, have arranged periods of rest for them in the regular series of festivals instituted in their honor." The Greeks agreed so fully with this reasoning that they increased these rest intervals to a point where they almost equaled the work periods. In Athens, there were more than eighty days of the year taken up by festivals and spectacles.

These spectacles and games were not the useless diversion of a lazy crowd like the plebs of Rome under the Caesars; they were part of religion and a national worship; they were the great school of patriotism and art, and even morality; "The Muses", said Plato, "and Apollo, their leader, preside over them

Various details of famous low reliefs. Top left, Herakles fighting the Amazons (London, British Museum). Bottom, depiction of a hoplite *(Athens, National Museum). Above, the Panathenaea (Athens, Parthenon).*

and celebrate with us." Criminals were banished, but the poor, even slaves, attended. At the great Dionysia in Athens, prisoners' chains were removed so that they too could celebrate the joyous festival of the god who chased away consuming sadness and rendered mans' mind as free as his words. As long as it lasted, no slave had a master, no captive a guardian. In Crete on Hermes' days, it was the masters who served their slaves at table.

Each city had its own festivals and reserved a certain number of places at these solemnities for the inhabitants of some allied city, colony or metropolis. As soon as the service to the god began, the city's business stopped; courts were closed; payments were postponed as were criminal executions, even in Sparta.

As in the Middle Ages in the West, organizations, professions, even ages and sexes had their patrons and their festivals. Thus in Athens, there were occasions for sailors, blacksmiths and undoubtedly many others; in Sparta, it was nurses; in other places, slaves. There were special patrons among the gods for youths, young girls and married women, and families had their saints, which did not prevent them from carrying out, on the altars of common gods, the ordinary rites for births, marriages and deaths.

"Formerly", said Plutarch, "the festival of Dionysus had a simplicity which did not exclude joy: at the head of the procession there was a pitcher full of wine crowned with vine branches; behind there was a he-goat and assistants holding a basket of figs; lastly, another assistant carried the *phallos,* symbol of fertility." Dionysus presided over the work of the fields, which in a country not rich in wheat, was above all the work of wine-growing. He was also, pre-eminently, the god of the grape, and each phase in the growing of the vine or the production of wine had a corresponding Dionysia. The coming grape-gathering was announced by a procession and games. The youths dressed in long, Ionian robes, carried vine plants with their clusters of grapes, and all the other fruits then ripe. And they sang: "Divine branches, from your boughs drip honey, oil and the pure nectar that fills the cup in which we find sleep." The festival ended in foot races; the prize for the winner was a vase of wine filled to the brim.

There was another festival when the grapes were put into the pressing vats. First there were libations and the most sumptuous feast possible — the participants took care to honor the god by consuming his gifts; next came a solemn procession. Half-drunk, they mounted chariots which had held the grape harvest, their heads hidden in vine branches, ivy or foliage, their bodies covered in animal skins or bizarre garments, then raced through the villages shouting gay comments. The Bacchantes or Maenads, women especially devoted to the god of fertility and bearing his name, formed a separate group, and held in their hands a thyrsus or *phallos*. In certain spots, trestles were set up. The procession stopped here; one of the assistants mounted the trestle to recite a dithyramb celebrating the adventures of the god of wine and joy. Choruses below answered, and Pans, Sylvans and Satyrs danced around them. Silenus on his donkey jeered and drank. A he-goat, the animal portrait of lasciviousness, was the reward for the one who composed the songs for the festival, which then served as a sacrifice on the altar of the god.

From these burlesque masquerades, obscene dialogues, pious and drunken songs, grew comedy and tragedy.

The Anthesteries, or festival of flowers, which lasted three days, took place in spring, after the fermentation, when the vases which held the new wine were first opened. A few drops were offered as a libation to the gods; for neighbors and slaves, the cup was filled to the brim.

These festivals were those of joy; the Bacchanalia were those of regret and sorrow. They took place at night, at the winter solstice, when the vine was dry and seemingly dead, showing that the god was far away or impotent. Single women, the Maenads or Furies, carried out these wild rites on the slopes of Parnassus and the peak of Taygetus, or in the plains of Macedonia and Thrace. Among the Dorians, these women showed some reserve; but in Boeotia, disheveled and half-naked, they ran along wildly in the gleam of torches and to the crash of cymbals, with savage cries, and violent gestures and delirium. The nervous excitement led to a complete disorder of the senses, ideas, words, and attitudes; obscenity became a pious act. When the Maenads danced wildly in dissolute movements, snakes wrapped around their arms, a dagger or thyrsus in hand, which they lashed around them, when drunkenness and the sight of blood carried the furious troop to delirium, it was the god who was acting in them, making them holy priestesses in his worship. And woe betide any man who happened to stumble across one of these mysteries: he, or an animal, was torn to pieces; they ate his quivering flesh and drank his blood.

This orgiastic cult was never very popular in Athens. The great solemnity in this city was, above, all the Panathenaic procession, which lasted four days, in the third year of each Olympiad, from the 25th to the 28th of the hecatombian month (July-August). It was both the festival of Athena and all the tribes of Attica, who, at the foot of her altar, were united into one people; it was also the festival of war and agriculture, and all the qualities of the body and the gifts of intelligence. In honor of the spear-carrying goddess, who had also created the olive tree and taught the arts to man, an armed dance was performed, as well as

Two typical statuettes from Tanagra.

chariot races and gymnastic wrestling matches, in which the victors' prizes were painted vases full of oil made from the sacred olive trees; equestrian exercises, in which horsemen carried lighted torches to the altar of Eros, the symbol of love which stimulated quickness of mind; then the recitation of verses by Homer or some other heroic poet, and musical contests; lastly, adding a holy and pure feeling to all those aroused by this solemn occasion, the citizen who had proved to be most worthy of his country was crowned in the presence of a vast throng drawn from all over Greece. For these grand Panathenaic processions, the time during which all work was suspended or even forbidden, in preparation for the festivities, was fifteen days.

Certain festivals remained popular for a very long time and are still the subject of much study: they include the mysteries, above all those of Samothrace and Eleusis, renowned as the oldest and most venerated.

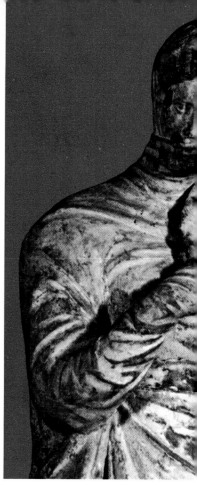

Unfortunately, our information is most incomplete, and we cannot follow the order of the ceremonies and mysteries, of which some were considered sacraments. The preliminary purifications, in which all dirt and impurity was removed are reminiscent of a baptism, and by drinking of the *cyceon* or holy beverage, the initiate communed with nature and life. Other rites consisted of the adoration of relics and mysterious objects which were held in the hand and kissed, passed from hand to hand, or which were put back into the holy basket, or *Kalathos.* "I have fasted", was the formula used in the mysteries; "I have drunk the *cyceon;* I have taken from the holy chest, and after having tasted, have replaced it in the basket; I have taken the basket and have put it in the holy chest."

There were three degrees of initiation, like three holy orders, since the initiates formed, in the original sense of the word, a clergy. The festivals were under the direction of the Eumolpides, to whom, says the poet, was given the golden key of the mysteries. On the 15th of the beodromian month, the head pontiff of Eleusis, the hierophant, who was always chosen from this family, and

who was a priest for life provided he remained celibate, went to the Poecile of Athens, wearing a diadem on his head and proclaimed the beginning of the solemnities, as well as the obligations of the initiates and those of the mystes (the novices who had been preparing themselves for a long while and received the initiation under the guidance of an Eumolpide). Barbarians and murderers, even involuntary ones, were excluded; but any man of Hellenic blood "with pure hands and soul", could be admitted. The following day, the members of the mysteries went to the sea for purifications, later repeated on the Eleusian road. On the 17th, 18th, and 19th the initiations were preceded by sacrifices, expiatory ceremonies and prayers, according to a ritual carefully kept secret from outsiders, and by a one-day fast, broken that evening.

The most touching of the ceremonies was the one in which a young boy or girl of pure Athenian blood, and who was called "the hearth child", because he remained the closest to the altar and the sacrificial flame, performed certain expiatory rites in the name of those asking to be admitted to the mysteries. It seemed that these supplications, spoken by innocent lips, would be more pleasant to the ears of the gods: the redemption of all by a child's prayer.

The 20th, the portion of the festival which took place in Athens was finished, and via the holy way, the procession left for Eleusis, carrying the image of Iacchos, who was being given as a son to Ceres, and whose name was joyfully shouted by the initiates. The road was only about ten thousand yards long, but many stops were made along the way for sacrifices.

In the evening they arrived at Eleusis, carrying torches, and they stayed there for several days; while the crowd turned its attention to a variety of entertainments, the initiates were totally engrossed in religious acts which were being performed for them alone. The herald, before opening the holy gates cried, "Go far from here, the unhallowed, the impious, magicians and murderers". Indeed, any such person, if found in the holy sanctuary among the initiates and mystery members, would have been punished by death. The same penalty, in addition to the confiscation of one's estate, was applied to those who revealed the mysteries.

The temple was on a hillside above Eleusis. A wall, which enclosed an area one hundred and thirty yards long and one hundred yards wide, kept unholy eyes from seeing and approaching the holy place. The initiates wore long, linen robes, and their hair was decorated with golden grasshoppers and myrtle crowns. The most holy rites were performed at night, a propitious time for mysterious things and the drunkenness of the mind born from the over-excited imagination. One of the most famous was the torch race. The initiates left the holy sanctuary, silently walking two by two, carrying a lighted torch, then entered the outer sanctuary, running in all directions, shaking the torches to throw sparks which would purify souls, switching torches from hand to hand signifying the communication and life-giving forces of light and the divine sciences. One by one the torches went out; and from the shadows came mysterious voices and terrifying images.

The mysteries were first meant for the eyes; they were religious drama much more than philosophical or moral teaching. But the mind could not remain unmoved by these moving ceremonies. Some stopped piously at what they had seen, going no further than the legend; others, few in number, went beyond the feeling to the idea, from imagination to reason, and thanks to the elasticity of the symbol, added, little by little, doctrines which were surely not there originally, or if they were, were most confused. Still later these ideas became better defined and a purified form of polytheism, not unlike Christian spirituality, came to be elaborated in the mysteries.

Diodorus Siculus believed that the initiation made better men.

In addition to the religiously inspired festivals or ceremonies, we must also acknowledge the importance of the celebrated Greek games: these collective demonstrations were equally important and characteristic of the spirit of people.

"The gods", said Pindar, "are the friends of the games". Greece had four games in which the entire nation participated: the Isthmian games near Corinth, in honor of Poseidon; the Nemean games in Argolis, which took place every two years; and those of Delphi and Olympia which eclipsed all others.

The *pentathlon* consisted of a series of five events in which a large field was gradually narrowed down. First an unspecified number of athletes competed in the long jump. Those who had covered the required distance were entered in the lists for the javelin. The four top men in this trial then raced, eliminating one of them. Thus there were three left for the discus and the last two for the wrestling match. Horse and chariot races were added, music and poetry contests, and all aroused the same enthusiasm. However, the music contest had only a small number of rather poor instruments available.

Neither gold, nor silver, nor brass was the coveted prize: the victor was rewarded with a crown of laurel or wild olive leaves. Yet, no matter which competition he was involved in, a young man—as well as his home town— counted it a supreme honor to win. On his return he was carried in a magnificent

Right, ancient gold piaster, possibly from Mycenae. Below, Satyric mask made of baked clay.

56

chariot; parts of walls were torn down to make way for him; he was exempt from taxes and was given the right to sit in the best place for all spectacles and games; his name was spoken everywhere; poets sang of him; painters and sculptors reproduced his image to decorate public places, avenues or the doors of temples. Fathers were known to die of joy upon embracing their victorious sons.

The Olympic games began at the full moon. Thus, these pleasures could continue on into the Greek night, more luminous than many days in northern climates.

Pericles was born in 494 B.C., four years before the first encounter between Greece and Asia. He had a beautiful body, and nature, as if to show his vast intelligence, had given him an inordinately large head, which is why artists were always careful to portray him wearing a helmet.

He moved not with sudden gestures, but with calm and serenity. Prudence, in its highest meaning, guided his conduct. For him, all was subject to thought. "Never," said Plutarch, "did he go before the tribunal without first

Above, cameo from the classical period.
Right, the Portland Vase: this famous piece, made of bluish glass, is adorned in cameo style.

praying to the gods not to allow him to utter a single word irrelevant to the subject he was discussing." He had studied physics and philosophy, meditated on government, but above all he studied the Athenians. No one was better acquainted with this people; no one saw its weaknesses more clearly, not in order to take advantage of them, but to remedy them.

As soon as he began to concern himself with affairs of State, he devoted himself to them completely; but so as not to be conspicuous, he rarely acted by himself, most often sending representative agents to appear in public places. His hand was felt but he was not seen.

One of his enemies, a base and evil man, followed him for an entire day, swearing at him on the public square, continuing his insults even as he followed him home; Pericles did not even turn around; but once at home, called a servant

to lead the man home by torchlight. He did not indulge in loud pleasures; he refused all invitations to feasts or festivals. He was never seen outside his house, if it was not to go a council or to the public square. In order not to divert his attention from the affairs of State by his own private fortune, and perhaps as well to make known his frugality, he had, each year and at the same time, all the products of his land sold; and each day he had purchased at the market whatever was needed for the maintenance of his household, which was ruled with economic severity. But he was not a man of sad or savage temperament; for pleasure he received a few friends and relaxed from work, discussing art with Phidias, literature with Euripides and Sophocles, and philosophy with Protagoras, Anaxagoras or Socrates. The Milesian Aspasia, the link in this group of extraordinary minds, added to her questions an inimitable grace which even more than her beauty, charmed Socrates and had seduced Pericles.

The people had at last found a leader they could admire and not fear. They also had unlimited confidence in him. Never had any man had such power in Athens. Without any special title, without specific authority, "and only by the authority of his genius and virtues", Pericles was master, more nobly than Augustus of Rome, master of Athens for fifteen years.

One must represent the Athenians of this time not like the plebs of Rome, who cared only about bread and games, but as an aristocracy elevated by its tastes, its elegance, its intellectual sophistication and its custom of authority, above the ordinary position of other peoples. The populace in Athens included slaves, foreigners, metics, this crowd of more than one hundred thousand souls crowding the city and Piraeus; the aristocracy was fifteen to twenty thousand citizens who alone judged and legislated, who appointed men from among their own ranks to occupy positions of public trust, and decided the fate of half of Greece.

Wealth came from trade, industry and banking, which redistributed it among a very large number of citizens; it was in fact so well distributed that Isocrates could say: "There is no one so poor that he must shame the State by begging."

Athens now had a flourishing industry, and its arms, metalwork, furniture and leather excelled all similar products on the market; its pottery went as far as Gades (Cadiz); its art objects, fabrics and books went everywhere. Fish and wine were imported from the islands; purple and glassware came from Tyre; Phoenician shipowners went far to search for tin; papyrus came from Egypt; gold, iron, wool and fabrics came from the Asian coast; grains, leathers, tar, rope, construction wood and numerous slaves came from the lands bordering the Hellespont and the Euxine or Black Sea. Trade, protected on all Greek waters by the naval fleet, was so active that Isocrates called Piraeus "the market-place of all Greece". And it was, not only by the merchants' choice, but by virtue of treaties and laws as well. Other tradesmen committed themselves to send certain merchandise only to that port, and an Athenian could acquire an interest in a boat leaving Piraeus only on the condition that the ship would return with cargo.

A writer has left us a description of the habits of the people of Piraeus: "You would think that you had been transported to one of our great maritime cities, since you have the same kinds of contracts, the same frauds, the same dangers one meets up with here."

Athens had a strong currency, in demand everywhere. "In most cities,", said Xenophon, "money has a value only locally, and consequently, merchants are forced to exchange their provisions for others. But Athens is different: its drachmas are accepted everywhere." In order to increase the power of credit, counterfeiters were punished by death. The silver trade was also very active. There were investing companies and money lenders who drew dividends. Bankers made loans using securities or precious objects as collateral; they had their account books in which they wrote debit and credit entries, their correspondence, and if not a bill of exchange, at least the check. Though lacking official status, the bankers were the trustees of documents and contracts. They made loans to the cities and in a manner underwrote loans to the State. Lastly it must be added that the republic taxed only 2 %, ad valorem; that its trade tribunals disposed of all litigation in winter; that the severity of legislation on debts guaranteed the execution of contracts; and finally that the high price of silver which was loaned at times at the rate of 18 %, and even higher, enabled capital-holders to rapidly amass a fortune.

Can man grow in the midst of such prosperity? It is not certain...

Aristophanes represents Athens exchanging the good old-fashioned habits for a ruinous luxury. The two peoples, those of Solon and the contemporaries, are personified by the simple, good-natured Strepsiade, and by his son Phidippide, who is ruining him with horses; the father is merely a machine for paying his son's debts. Awakened at night by the troubles they are causing him, he tosses nervously in bed, suddenly hearing Phidippide in his sleep speak of

horses and expenses. "Oh," cries the poor old father, "now what have I lost?" Strepsiade was a good farmer, happy far from the city; but then luxury and civilization began to fascinate him; everyone rushes to it only to get burnt, like the moth and the flame. "Ah," cries Strepsiade, addressing his sleeping son, "damn the day I married your mother. I was leading a happy life in the fields, common, unpolished, inelegant, surrounded by bees, sheep, olives. Then I took it into my head to marry Megacles' niece, me, a country fellow, and a city woman, pompous, loving luxury, raised at Caesyra's school. When I came close to her, she smelled the wine on me, and the odor of baskets of fruit and piles of wool; she, all perfumed with unguents and saffran, spoke only of expenses, entertainments, feasts. I cannot say that she did nothing, for she did weave cloth, and I, showing her this coat said to her, "M'love, you're weaving too tightly". Then this son comes along. And she takes him tenderly to her breast, saying to him: "When will you be big enough to drive a chariot to the city, like Megacles, wearing a saffron-colored coat?" And I for my part said to him. "When will you be big enough to lead the goats, like your father, dressed in an animal skin?" But he didn't listen to me, and he let his horses loose on my fortune".

Pericles wanted all citizens to be guaranteed a subsistence income. The poorest were sent to the many colonies he founded, where they became landowners. As for those who stayed in the city, they found ample resources by working in the arsenals and on construction projects begun by Pericles, in the

trade which was based in Athens, in the indemnity of one obolus given to judges and all men of the population who attended the assemblies; lastly, in military service, which paid very well. Thanks to the gentle climate, the Athenian did not have to spend as much as northerners on clothing, food and lodging. Free distribution of grains, not periodically as in Rome, and sacrifices, at the expense of the State, where as many as three hundred cattle and five hundred goats were immolated, helped provide for the welfare of the people.

Athens had to be worthy of its people and its empire. In order to embellish it with immortal monuments, Pericles did not hesitate to use money from the treasuries of its allies. His view was that, as long as Athens provided efficient protection, it could not be held accountable to anyone. The people and the city benefited from this ethically lax approach. A mass of workers in all industries found a means of employing their hands and earning an honorable living; there were professions organized by leaders for quarrying and cutting marble, casting bronze, working the gold, ivory, ebony and cedar used in the construction of public buildings or statues of the gods, for sculpting the rich ornamentation of temples or decorating them with brilliant paintings.

This is Pericles' description of the industrial activities of the Athenians: "We buy stone, brass, ivory, gold, ebony, cypress; and innumerable workers, carpenters, masons, blacksmiths, stone cutters, dyers, goldsmiths, embroiderers, turners, cabinet-makers, painters, put them to creative use. Shipowners, sailors and pilots bring an immense quantity of materials by sea; carriers and drivers bring them by land; wheelwrights, cord-makers, stone-cutters, harness-makers, pavers, work them; each boss, like a general in the army, has around him a troop of subordinate artisans, with no specific profession, whom he can use as a reserve whenever necessary."

Pericles handed the supreme responsibility for these works over to Phidias who, like Alexander, had in turn extremely capable lieutenants under him. The Parthenon, or Virgin's Temple, entirely of Pentelican marble, also called the *Hecatombedon,* because of the length of its *cella* (100 Greek feet), was the work of Ictinus. Coroebos began the temple of Eleusis, one of the largest in Greece. Callicrates directed the construction of a third wall which cut into two zones the long, wide avenue leading to Athens from the sea, in such a way that if the enemy seized one, the other remained free, permitting communications between the city and the ports.

The Milesian Hippodamos founded Piraeus, the first city in Greece built on a regular plan, and also the first whose commercial prosperity and defense were assured by great and costly works. Inscriptions found at Piraeus show that the maritime arsenal contained berths for 372 ships.

The *Odeon,* which was designed for musical contests, was built on the model of the tent of Xerxes and the Erechtheion was rebuilt; this was the principal work in the Ionic order, just as the Parthenon is the masterpiece of the Doric order. The magnificent vestibule of the Acropolis, the Propylaea, all in marble, costing 2,012 talents, more than the Republic's annual revenue, was the work of Mnesicles.

And yet, there was grumbling about the considerable sums of money used for these works. The rich above all complained of a lavishness that was destroying the treasury, and invoked the rights of the allies whose tributes were being used to "gild and embellish the city like a coquettish woman one covers

with precious gems, and to erect magnificent statues and build temples, one of which alone cost 1,000 talents". But of course Pericles silenced them with a word. "Athenians", he said one day to the entire assembly, "do you find that I am making too many expenditures?" "Yes", was the reply from everywhere. "Well then", he answered, "it shall be I who shall bear them; but also, as is fair, it will be my name alone which will be carved on all these monuments".

These words must not be taken too seriously, since Pericles would never have been able to place 1,000 talents in the treasury; but the feeling attributed to the people is true. Soon enough a patriotic pride animated this people, proud of its beautiful city. Each citizen, even the most obscure, felt himself important, not seeing any difference between the education of the rich and the poor. He listened to the most clever orators; he discussed a question of art with Phidias and adjudicated the contests of tragedies between Sophocles and Euripides. Every day the Athenian saw his ships leave from Piraeus, some for the Euxine, others for Thrace and Egypt; still others set sail for the Adriatic or the coasts of Italy and Sicily. And glancing at the sea around him, his domain, he saw in the monuments of Athens a fitting reflection of the grandeur of the empire. Indeed, Athens was Minerva's city, intelligence armed.

Through the events in its history, Athens had acquired the character of a democratic society; it was then necessary, via a broad public education system, to diminish the differences of intellectual cultivation which existed among the citizens, so that moral equality could guarantee political equality. Pericles instituted musical competitions for the Panathenaea, those solemn festivals attended by the entire population of Attica, in which runners, athletes and poets came to compete for the crown of honor offered by the Republic, and where a law ordered that the poems of Homer be read to the people, as well as the Perseides of Chaerilos, the slave from Samos, poet of victory and liberty who, it

Left and right, characteristic ornamentation on vases of the classical period: one on a red background, and the other on a black background.

Following pages: a) this superb scene appears on a classical vase with a black background; b) vase with black background, showing royal figure, and cup for wine (3rd century BC).

was said, was given by Athenae a gold piece for each of his verses. Xenophon said that Pericles increased the city festivals to a point where there were more in Athens than in any other city in Greece, eighty each year; not eighty days of laziness or debauchery, but great national solemnities, during which the pleasures of the mind mingled with the spectacle of religious pomp, the most perfect art in the loveliest natural settings. Thus painters, orators and poets united to revive glorious and revered memories; and where the theatre, despite satiric drama and comedy, was, in the works of the great tragedians, a school for morality.

Dramatic presentations were primarily, in Athens as in Rome and medieval Europe religious festivals. It was believed that the prosperity of the city made it essential that the solemnities be celebrated with a magnificence pleasing to the gods. Spectators at the theatre, like the faithful at the altar, felt that they were performing a holy act. The theatre of Bacchus had been constructed in such a way that it could accomodate the entire population. Theatrical presentations were a liturgical institution. This can be seen even in the sauciest plays of Aristophanes, where between two obscenities one heard a chaste prayer.

Below, wedding procession (5th century BC). Right, realistic scene depicting a young man apparently wooing the lady of his choice.

Thus in the midst of these glorious demonstrations of thought and art, the place of honor was justly given to dramatic poetry, the most magnificent flowering of the Athenian genius.

The first in time to urge man's spirit toward a superior ideal was Aeschylus, whose dramas have the twin character of powerful works: simplicity and grandeur. The poet was also a valiant soldier, a fine citizen and a believer. His work is moved by both patriotic and religious enthusiasm.

Aeschylus said of his dramas that they were no more than the leftovers from the great Homeric banquet: he was right. His tragedies, true epic fragments, have a deep brilliance and mysterious majesty; a formidable divinity, Destiny, moves throughout them, silent and invisible, followed by Nemesis, divine jealousy, which allows no human grandeur to go beyond a certain fixed limit; both fill the spectator's soul with poignant emotions and superstitious terrors.

Sophocles was almost the same age as Pericles, since his birth is placed around 498, more probably 495; he was also a contemporary of Aeschylus, thirty years older than Euripides, and fifteen years younger than Herodotus, whom he celebrates in a poem. He had been chosen at Salam, because of his great beauty, to lead the chorus of adolescents who sang, while dancing around the trophy, the victory hymn; he lived until 406, which made him nearly ninety years old at death, just under the number of tragedies he wrote. Thus he saw all the greatness of Athens, as well as the beginning of its decline.

It is said that towards the end of his life, his son Iophon wanted to have him confined, saying that he was no longer in complete possession of his faculties. In defense Sophocles read to the judges a description of Attica that he had just written at the age of eighty-nine. Travelers find that it is still precise, but no translation can truly render its harmonious grace; here are several lines: "Stranger, you have come to the most beautiful place on earth, the land of swift horses, where the nightingale sings its melodies among the sacred foliage, sheltered from the sun's fire and winter's cold. Here Bacchus wanders with the nymphs, his divine maidens; and under the heavenly dew forever flourishes the narcissus, the crown of great goddesses, and golden saffron..."

Sophocles, in Œdipus Rex, shows love without ever daring to speak of it and gives women a position denied them by Aeschylus. Many heroes had been celebrated by the epic muse and on Pindar's lyre. Opposite the valiant men, Sophocles puts Antigone, equal to them in courage and surpassing them in devotion.

The subject of the Trachinian Women is the death and apotheosis of Hercules. This poem would be of little interest without the role of Dejanira, a women devoted to the hero, and sympathetic to the unhappy situation of the captives, even when she finds a rival among them. She does not loathe young Iole with jealousy, but accuses her of love: "Eros conquers even the gods, as he conquered, me, and so why not another as well? I would be mad to accuse my husband if he is struck with this pain, or this woman who has done me no injustice. For her I have a most profound pity, seeing how her beauty has undone her."

Euripides, born, according to Aristophanes of an inn-keeper and herb-seller (480 B.C.), had the hard life and extremely touchy personality of the self-made man who does not achieve his wishes: at home, quarrels and repudiation, and never a smile on his sad face; in the theatre, rare applause, sometimes

Two Greek figures, the work of an émigré potter living in Etruria, highly typical of their kind.

Above and opposite, assorted faces, portrayed with striking realism.

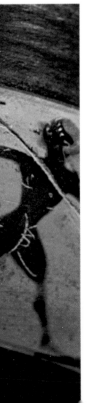

outright revolt, and of ninety plays presented, only four victories; Aristophanes as an adversary; a horrible death in the jaws of dogs; and as a last iniquity or even a curse, a poisonous spring running near his tomb in Macedonia. And yet Euripides was a great poet and the most popular of the Greek tragedians.

In the general history of the theatre, two periods can be established: in the first, the mysteries or religious drama; in the second, human drama. Euripides belongs to the second; he initiated modern theatre by bringing to the stage his contemporaries with ancient titles, combining them with eternal passions. A characteristic trait of his tragedy is the position he gives to women and to love: it is the heart of all his dramas. His Phaedra, the victim of Aphrodite, is the ancestress of all those stirred, charmed or tortured by Eros. His two wives must have caused him such sadness in life that he got revenge in his theatre, with such bitterness against their sex that he was called the misogynist; and yet several of his heroines have become immortal for their devotion and sacrifices. Euripides can be forgiven for having written that woman is the most shameless of all animals.

Comedy, which was born with its sisters, tragedy, in the Dionysian festivals was in the hands of Aristophanes a weapon for combat, striking especially science and philosophy, the bravest generals, the greatest orators and the wisest men. The only thing this comedian did not laugh at was himself.

Listen to this dialogue between Demosthenes and the butcher who, according to the oracles, was destined to govern Athens, and whom the conservatives want to run against Cleon:

"*Demosthenes:* Are you of respectable birth?

Butcher: By the gods, certainly not! I come from the riffraff.

Demosthenes: A lucky man! How well everything is working out for you.

Butcher: But I have absolutely no education, except that I know the letters of the alphabet fairly well.

Demosthenes: Ah, beware! Knowing the alphabet fairly well could be harmful. The Republic wants neither a wise man nor a respectable man for the

High jinks after a dinner party: the women are dancing, and so are the men (some of them with other men); on the right, erotic Bacchanalian rounds.

government. It needs a dunce and a rogue."

And these replies:

"*Chremylus:* Are you a laborer?

The Sycophant: Do you think I'm mad?

Chremylus: A merchant?

The Sycophant: I use the word when it's convenient.

Chremylus: But don't you have a trade?

The Sycophant: No, by Jupiter.

Chremylus: Then what do you live on, if you do nothing?

The Sycophant: I keep an eye on public and private affairs."

It should be noted that there were now two basic groups in the population of the city: the old Athenians, including the surviving remnants of the aristocracy, who, though too weak to rule, could nonetheless have helped contain the situation; and the populace, who had been drawn to Piraeus in droves by war and the shipping trade. The latter group, a restless, envious and half-starved mob, wanted to live off enemy booty, extortions from the allies and fines and confiscations imposed on the rich. When assembled in the Agora, these two groups became one single people, and the second, its ranks swollen by the numbers of poor people in the city itself, was dominant. It was the group which legislated, administered and judged—and it was none too choosy about the merits of the men it took for its leaders: from Pericles it stooped to Cleon, from Cleon to Hyperbolos, from him to Syracosios, and any glib talker capable of flattering its prejudices soon became an important person.

Aristophanes was too much the son of his century not to be influenced by all of this. He was thoroughly imbued with the prevailing atmosphere; and this extreme conservative, this lover of times past was the boldest freethinker of his day. He called for the return of the old ways, while at the same time working to destroy whatever remained of them.

Faith in oracles, as we know, was very close to the Greek heart, even in frivolous Athens. Aristophanes made fun of it, and gave prophets and soothsayers a very hard time. One of them, the Boeotian Bacis, whose life is now lost in the darkness and mist of legend, was very much in favor. His so-called hexameters were collected, and people used to read them to find the decrees of Fate—just as the Romans were later to do with the books of Sibyl. According to the poet, Cleon had laid in quite a store of them. While he was sleeping, Nicias stole the oracles from him. But the Paphlagonian had a trunkful, and the butcher two whole roomsful.

"*Demos:* What do they speak of?

Cleon: Of Athens, Pylos, you, me, everything.

Demos (to the Butcher): And yours?

Butcher: Athens, lentils, Lacedaemonians, fresh mackerel, you, me.

Demos: Well! Read them to me, especially the one I like so much where it says that I will be an eagle soaring among the clouds."

Then follows a grotesque parody of the replies "which the august Delphic oracles made to reverberate in Apollo's sanctuary".

According to the poet's acid version of events, thanks to the mysteries doctrines were spread far and wide, sending virtuous souls winging towards the regions of light and the abode of the gods, to become, along with the others, incorruptible and imperishable beings. Shooting stars were really rich men

Below, small vase with mounted figure; note the particularly refined shapes. Right, the superb ornamentation of another vase, showing a young man playing the lyre.

leaving a banquet, holding a lantern in their hand; after all, merrymaking also went on in the celestial regions; in fact they also had their own houses of loose virtue, not unlike those on earth.

Plato, being an enemy of democracy, naturally throught much of the writer who fought it so valiantly. In the *Symposium,* he placed him next to Socrates. This surprising eulogy is Plato's: "The Graces, looking for an indestructible sanctuary, found the soul of Aristophanes."

The Greeks did not immediately achieve the architectural perfection which we admire on the Acropolis. For their first dwelling places they had given the gods mountain-tops and deep forests; but they wanted them to be nearer, and from the earliest times began constructing simple, rustic abodes which gradually came to be embellished and attracted the other arts.

They knew neither the pointed arch nor the dome. At one time it seemed that these features were present in structures found at Tiryns and Mycenae; yet the truth of the matter is that, if bays and galleries end in pointed forms, it is simply because the courses of stone gradually converged and met at the top. This method is thus crude and barbaric; it was later replaced by the flat-molding and the pediment.

All Greek temples have a similar general layout; and yet the architectonic combinations are numerous, on account of the nature of the different materials used and the ornamentation that decorates them, the number of columns and the width of the intercolumniations which determines the building's proportions, above all the special nature of each of the three orders, Doric, Ionic and Corinthian. A single element of construction, the column with the part of the entablature it supports, determines this special character.

The Parthenon, built entirely of Pentelican marble, is not the largest of Greek temples, but its execution is the most perfect, and it is this feature that makes it the masterpiece of Hellenic art.

The interior of the Parthenon was made up of two chambers: the smaller one behind, called the *opisthodome,* contained the public treasury; the larger, or *cella,* held the statue of the goddess born without mother, but from the thoughts of the head of the gods, and was like the soul, whose material shell was the Parthenon. Figures in round-relief, approximate twice life-size, decorated the two pediments of the temple. The frieze which ran around the *opisthodome* and the *cella,* thirteen yards above their floor, was more than 160 yards long, and represented the great Panathenaic processions.

The monument was finished in 435. It was neither the centuries nor barbarians who mutilated it. The Parthenon was still nearly intact when in 1687, on the 27th of September, Morosini bombarded the citadel. A projectile, setting on fire several casks of powder in the temple, blew up part of it; the Venetian then wanted to remove the statues from the pediment and broke them. Lord Elgin, at the beginning of the 19th century, removed the bas-reliefs of the frieze and the metopes: it was another disaster.

An observation has been made about the Parthenon which shows the profundity of the Greek sense of art, and their remarkable ability to correct geometry with taste. In the Parthenon there is not one perfectly flat surface. Thus the beauty of the columns is in part due to a slight swelling towards the middle, which the eye does not perceive as such; and both the colonnades and walls lean slightly towards the center of the building, directed towards an invisible

Ancient vases and amphora.

meeting point somewhere in the clouds; and lastly, all horizontal lines are convex. All this with such precision! Just enough so that the eye and light gently flow over the surfaces and the monument has at the same time the grace of art and the solidity of strength.

Herodotus recorded a typically Greek fact for us: after his death, Philip of Crotona was revered as a hero in a small public building constructed for him, having been the handsomest man of his time, and the historian agrees with the Aegisthians who created this special god. Nor does he question if Xerxes had truly royal qualities: "In his entire army", said Herodotus, "no one was more worthy of sovereign power by his beauty than he". In one of the choruses in which he was often the prize-winner because of his magnificence, Nicias had given the role of Dionysus to a young slave, so perfect in his beauty and so nobly costumed, that upon seeing him, the temple burst into applause. Nicias immediately made him a free man, believing, he said, that it was impious to keep in servitude a man who had been hailed by the Athenians in the figure of a god.

From its first to last day, Greece thought this way. Often in the Odyssey, Ulysses and Telemachus think they have seen a god when they happen to meet a tall and handsome man; and the cold, severe Aristotle says: "If there were born mortals who looked like gods, all men would agree to swear them eternal allegiance."

These memories explain the divine honors bestowed upon Antinous by the most Greek of Roman emperors, but they also show how the worship of beauty, which the Greeks had made into a religion and whose theory was

Below and right, two realistic scenes: a burial and the laying out of a dead body. It is thought to be the body of Achilles surrounded by the Nereids — hence the curious face at the foot of the bed, his shield.

formulated by Plato, formed the artists of Greece, and to a certain extent its philosophers.

The Greeks understood the dance very differently from the way we do, giving it great respect and attention. For them the dance was part of religious ceremonies and military education. "The ancients", said Plato in the seventh book of *Laws,* "have left us a great number of beautiful dances". In Dorian cities they were a necessary part of the worship of Apollo, and the most revered and serious people took part in them.

Plato, in his *Laws,* which is a kind of commentary on the customs and legislation of the Athenians, attaches great importance, even in the moral education of the young, to the need for the ephebes to know "the art of choruses", including song and dance. "These divinities who preside over our solemnities", he writes, "give us a feeling for order, precision and harmony; and this feeling which, under their guidance, regulates our movements, teaches us to create, by our songs and dances, a bond which runs among us and unites us". Far from dreading these exercises which at other times served merely for pleasure, the poet-philosopher regarded them as necessary to the good order of cities and souls.

In Sparta and Athens the pyrrhic was a military exercise and patriotic instruction. The ephebes danced it at the great and lesser Panathenaea, imitating all the movements of a battle, to attack, defend or avoid being hit.

At this time, each Greek people did not have as its leader a man like Pericles, whose name may fairly be given to the period we are considering, but those who did not actually contribute to the arts and humanities at least understood them, and by their enthusiasm inspired artists and poets.

Plataea requested of Phidias a colossus of Athena and a statue of Zeus; Lemnos wanted a statue of Minerva, called by antiquity "the beautiful Lemnian"; Delphi wanted a Diana and an Apollo; and Olympia the statue of Jupiter which rendered to the eye the majesty of the master of the gods. Delphi and Corinth instituted painting competitions.

Having lived for many years along the outer edges of their civilization, the Greek philosophers eventually converged on its center. Starting with the age of Pericles, Athens became their battleground: it was here that theories vied with one another; here began the revolution which led paganism into a period of decadence for the people, and of moral transformation for superior men. The spirit was removed from the ancient religion in two ways. The mysteries, specially those of Eleusis, had little by little released, united and developed the spiritual elements contained in the old cults, and without breaking from polytheism, they put forth the idea of a single god. Stronger and freer, the philosophers, through reason alone, retraced the steps to an initial creator. But by stirring up the great problems that religion had supposedly solved, these men naturally caused insubordination and revolt against it.

While they thus undermined the national religion by reason, the comic poets killed it by mockery, and their influence rapidly spread in a country where everyone read even when traveling. What must the crowds of Athenian theatre-

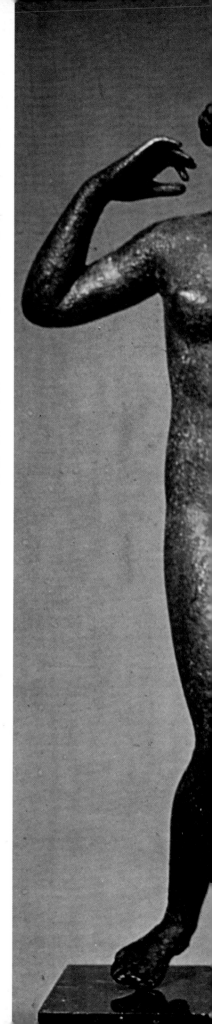

Two specimens of the art of bronze sculpture: a statuette of Aphrodite and, on the right, one of Poseidon.

goers have felt as they saw the gods treated with such irreverence by Aristophanes in *Plutus, The Birds* and *The Frogs?*

Art did its share in this work of destruction. Parodies of the gods were depicted on painted vases, samples of which were found everywhere, filling the role of our newspapers and caricatures, while popularizing the irreverent Olympic scenes that the comic poets had brought to the stage.

A certain number of these still exist in collections. One of them, in the Vatican, shows Jupiter at Amphitryon's door, hidden by a bearded mask, and holding a ladder which would enable him to reach, like some common libertine in an amorous adventure, the window where Alcmena awaits him. Near him, Mercury, disguised as a pot-bellied slave, is going to help the lovers escape by lighting the way with a lantern. Another vase, in the British Museum, shows Bacchus who has gotten Vulcan intoxicated in order to take him, despite his protests, to Olympia, where he needs help. On another vase it is Poseidon, Hercules and Mercury who are fishing to supply food for the gods' feast.

Aristophanes attacked sophistry with unique energy, without proposing another solution except going backwards three generations. But didn't he himself have all the vices of the times? The true solution was not an unawareness of past times; it was to be found rather in the virile intellectual discipline just begun by a certain man, and this man was the one whom the poet had most cruelly attacked.

Socrates was born in 469, of a midwife named Phenarete, and a sculptor named Sophronisces. He was quite ugly, which helped him learn quite soon that only moral ugliness is repulsive. It is said that he first exercised his father's profession.

Indifferent to all external matters as no other Greek had ever been, to the point of having left Athens of his own accord only once or twice, he concerned himself with man's interior life, and spent his days looking within himself and others. The purpose of his life was to convert a few souls to virtue and truth. Armed with two powerful weapons, that of a clear and sharp intelligence which quickly discovered error, and subtle and strong logic which irretrievably bound his adversary, he made it his duty to track down falsehood. And he fulfilled this mission for forty years, with the faith of an apostle and the pleasure of an artist, delighting in his victories over presumption or ignorance. Didn't he even one day make Theodotus, the beautiful courtesan, know that there were means available to her to render her profession more lucrative?

This teaching at all times and with all people was neither theoretical nor preparatory; it went on from day to day, in any place and any time a falsehood became evident. Although he was an assiduous observer of the public scene, he took part in public affairs only when the law obliged him to do so, he was on the lookout to stop any false doctrine, seizing it and revealing what it hid, its emptiness. He was always seen walking in the city, this man disfavored by nature with his flat nose, thick lips, short, thick neck, a protruding belly like Silenus, round, bulging eyes, though these were lit by his genius. He roamed here and there, sometimes distracted, absorbed in deep meditations, staying in the same spot for twenty-four hours at a time, it was said; often approaching a passer-by, or entering a shop to discuss with the artisan the subject that seemed suitable to him. He was forever carrying on dialogues. From a simple fact, to which his interlocutors readily assented, he made them draw unexpected consequences,

Left, a two-faced stele (3rd century BC) — not the head of Janus, however, as there is a male figure on one side and a female figure on the other. Above, the Apollo of Piraeus (6th century BC). Below, bronze male figure with inlaid eyes. Following pages, an earring with pendant.

and inexorably led them, without seeming to intervene himself, to ideas which they had not anticipated at all. His method became famous in antiquity under the name of *Socratic irony*; it taught one to think and to assure oneself that one was thinking correctly. He also called himself, in memory of his mother's profession, the midwife of the mind, leading the artisan, like himself, to develop more elevated and rational ideas on art, politics, affairs of State, sophistry, and the questions he himself raised. A bit of jesting was always part of his conversations. Socrates interested himself only in the man in search of truth, a seeker, as he said; at first he pretended to have great faith in his adversary's knowledge, seeming to want to learn from him; little by little the roles changed, and most often he reduced him to absurdity or silence.

How could this just man have been condemned to the tortures reserved for traitors and murderers? There were three charges against him: Socrates did not recognize the Republic's gods; he introduced new divinities, and he corrupted youth.

We love Greece for its poets, philosophers and artists, but also because it was the first culture in the ancient world whose ideal was political liberty guaranteed by the most complete development of each citizen. The East knew only the calm and sterile unity of great monarchies subject to a single will, almost always the same, despite the diversity of those who wielded sovereign power. Greece was made up of as many independent states as the valleys and promontories given to it by Nature for its defense; and in almost all these communities, the inhabitants accepted the religion and constitutional law in exchange for a single freedom, that of decreeing themselves that law which governed them.

One sentiment which one does not normally expect to find in these cities was charity. The age of the numerous institutions formed by Christianity had not yet arrived, as the current state of society did not yet require them. Demosthenes bought back captives' freedom, and gave dowries to poor girls, and he was not alone in doing this. He could say, as in his speech *On the Crown:* "You know, Athenians, that I have been affable, human, willing to help in any misfortune"; elsewhere he boasted of never having shirked his philanthropic duties; this word which we imagine to be modern, was in fact in current usage in Athens, more than twenty-three centuries ago. Lysias mentions another citizen who secretly gave dowries to girls, freed prisoners, and buried dead bodies found on the roads, asking no compensation or reward from anyone. And how many others did like him! If the payment given to those who attended the public assembly and religious festivals had political drawbacks, it had at first been given as a means of helping those who needed it. The same was true of the distributions of wheat to the people from time to time, and of the meals celebrated after the great sacrificial burnings, when the gods were satisfied merely by the smoke from the altar. Hippocrates asked doctors, in turn, to ask no payment from those who could not afford it, and many cities gave medical aid to the poor; lastly, Plato wrote: "We must do harm to no man, not even the malicious one."

Naturally, between the shepherd, simple worshipper of Pan of Arcadia, and the elegant citizen of Athens, there were great differences; but there were even greater similarities. In addition to the same language and religion, there was a moral communion. The horizon of one was immense, that of the other limited; but both saw similar things and rejected what they found in contemporary

Above, ornamental detail on a vase showing an elegant lady from the classical period.
Right, this very refined piece of jewelry dates from the 4th century BC.

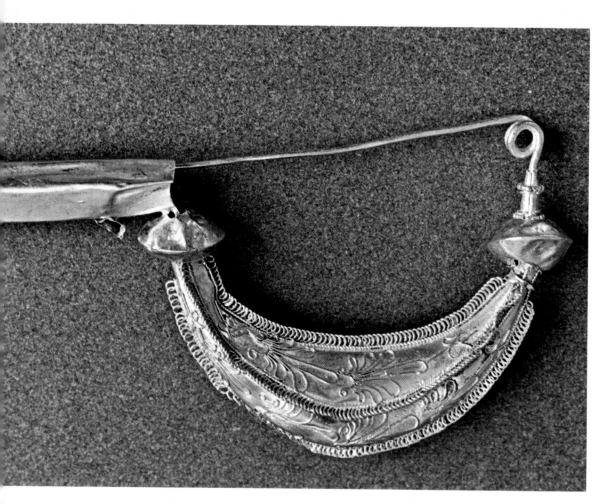

Above, gold fibula (5th century BC).

nations: human sacrifice, mutilation, polygamy, the sale of children by their father, as found in Thrace and even Rome, and the servile obeisance of an Asian for his Great King. Both fought naked in the public games, though most barbarians, according to Plato and Herodotus, would have regarded such conduct as quite indecent. Lastly Homer's poems, sung from one end of Hellas to the other, served as holy scripture for them, creating the idealized nation protected by panhellenic Zeus.

Thus there is a Greek people distinct from the barbarians, but as well, as Herodotus says, a Hellenic body which indicates the Greek race, later to signify civilization.

The magnificence of the Hellenic life lasted no longer than a century and a half, but this short time was enough to make Greece the holy land of civilization: human thought was born there.

It is not, as an envious Roman said, because Greece produced great and clever writers that it earned an immortal reputation. This small country changed, in the moral order, the poles of the earth. The East had given birth to wise men, but under them the people were no more than docile flocks, ruled by the master's voice. In Greece, for the very first time, humanity became conscious of itself.

94